7 Great Turning Projects
for the Smaller

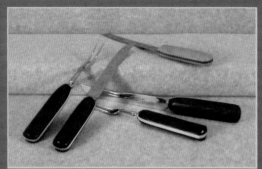

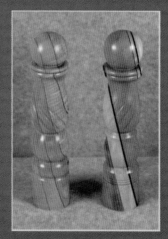

Bill Bowers

Schiffer Publishing Ltd®

4880 Lower Valley Road Atglen, Pennsylvania 19310

Dedication

To My Daughter Suzanne

Designed by John P. Cheek
Cover Design by Bruce Waters
Type set in Zurich BT

ISBN: 978-0-7643-2726-1
Printed in China

Published by Schiffer Publishing Ltd.
4880 Lower Valley Road
Atglen, PA 19310
Phone: (610) 593-1777; Fax: (610) 593-2002
E-mail: Info@schifferbooks.com

For the largest selection of fine reference books on this and related subjects, please visit our web site at
www.schifferbooks.com
We are always looking for people to write books on new and related subjects. If you have an idea for a book please contact us at the above address.

This book may be purchased from the publisher.
Include $3.95 for shipping.
Please try your bookstore first.
You may write for a free catalog.

In Europe, Schiffer books are distributed by
Bushwood Books
6 Marksbury Ave.
Kew Gardens
Surrey TW9 4JF England
Phone: 44 (0) 20 8392-8585; Fax: 44 (0) 20 8392-9876
E-mail: info@bushwoodbooks.co.uk
Website: www.bushwoodbooks.co.uk
Free postage in the U.K., Europe; air mail at cost.

Contents

Proem..4

Chapter 1. Scoops..5

Chapter 2. Turned Cylinder Box.........................14

Chapter 3. Off-Centered Handles......................23

Chapter 4. Lidded Bowls with Foil Leaf............31

Chapter 5. Christmas Ornaments.....................40

Chapter 6. Pepper and Salt Mills.....................47

Chapter 7. Gallery..56

Acknowledgments..64

Proem

While attempting to complete a book on projects for the smaller lathe it became rather obvious too much material was present for a single text. The easiest solution was to divide the projects into two books, the first consisting of ten easy projects geared to the beginning turner and a second with seven, more complicated endeavors that the intermediate turner or those who had completed the first book could readily accomplish. As with the first book all projects can be completed on a mini-lathe or one of the standard 12-36 inch lathes during a weekend. A bed extension for the mini-lathe is once again required especially to easily complete the salt and peppermills. For turning off-centered handles additional weight needs to be added to mini or light weight lathes. This can be accomplished with sand bags, concrete blocks, or lead shot on an added shelf or laid across the mini lathe's legs. A heavy friend out of harms way standing on the legs of the mini lathe is another method of stabilizing the machine.

As with the first project book the seven projects described herein originate from demonstrations given at Alaska Woodturners Association's monthly meetings and the stock utilized often is left-over or scrap lumber. Even last year's Christmas tree is of use for this year's ornaments. A January visit to the local Christmas tree dump may yield enough stock for many ornaments for the following year.

Chapter One details two projects, the first a Raffan-type scoop—end grain hollowing—and the second a Berger-type scoop—multi-axis turning. Chapter Two explains how to make a simple cylinder box with the correct proportions. Instructions on how to turn the top and bottom inside and outside, parallel and flush are described. Chapter Three demonstrates how to make off-centered short handles for kitchen cutlery. The technique should not be used for long tool handles on the mini-lathe or smaller lathes as too much vibration ensues and safety becomes an issue. Chapter Four gives a complete description on how to make small lidded bowls and apply various types of foil leaf. Chapter Five explains how to construct hollowed globes from recycled Christmas trees and turn captive ringed icicles with applied twists. Chapter Six details construction of crush grind salt and peppermills from laminated left-over lumber and displays how to add twists to embellish the end product. Chapter Seven has a gallery of finished products to entice the reader to try their own ideas at turning.

Equipment needed to accomplish the projects is described in the text, but most tools are standard turning tools with a few exceptions. A small band saw, table saw, chop saw, jointer, small planer, bench top belt sander and drill press are the power tools needed. Once again a dust-free finishing area is desirable.

One may start at any chapter and work through its project or at the beginning of the book following each chapter's instructions, but, most importantly, have fun and be careful. Remember to practice turning safety, wear eye protection, a dust mask, proper clothing, and comfortable hard-toed shoes, and remove jewelry or objects that could catch in the lathe. Remember, the exuberance experienced at the lathe is exceptional medicine for the soul.

Chapter 1
Scoops

There are basically two types of scoops, the Raffan scoop which is made by end grain hollowing, and the Berger scoop which is a multi-axis turned scoop. The former is easy to do but the latter requires much more skill and dexterity.

The stock selected comes from my friend Arnie's wood pile and is a 3 by 3 by 8 inch chunk of fir from an old pallet. Mount it between centers using the steb center and live center.

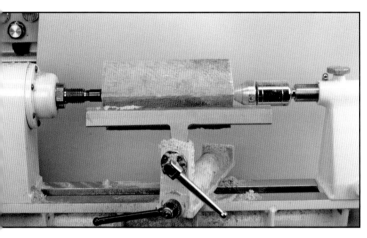

Begin turning it down to a cylinder using a roughing gouge.

Measuring with calipers, bring the cylinder down the proper diameter to fit the Talon chuck with #3 jaws. If the cylinder is too big cut a spigot to fit the jaws.

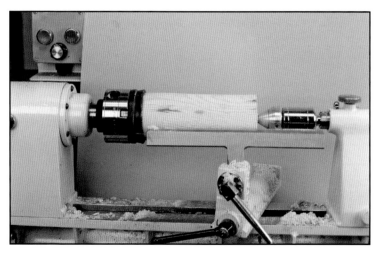

Mount the cylinder in the jaws with a really tight fit, as we will be end grain hollowing and need firm support. Don't worry about leaving marks on the stock.

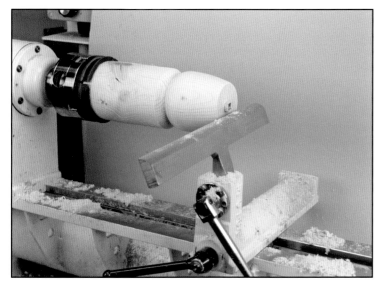

Turn a goblet or cup form, then back off the tailstock. Remember to leave a thick portion at the base of the cup so that no vibrations are created when hollowing out the cup. The complete cup shape can be turned after the cup is hollowed.

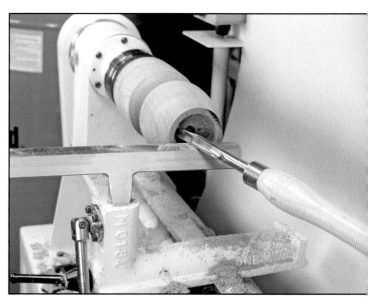

Sweep around from the center to the edge to make nice, controlled cuts with the flute opened to 45 degrees upon exit.

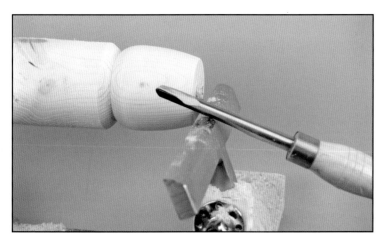

Using a modified ½-inch spindle gouge (this is a Ray Key end grain hollowing tool) begin to hollow out the cup.

Push in another inch and sweep around again until the cup is hollowed out.

Push in at dead center about one inch—the tool will act like a drill—to begin the hollowing. The tool must be parallel to the lathe bed to function properly.

It is a good idea to use a depth gauge to assess how deep one is going.

Set it so that whenever the thickness of the bottom is about ¼ inches, the depth gauge will rest on the cup's rim.

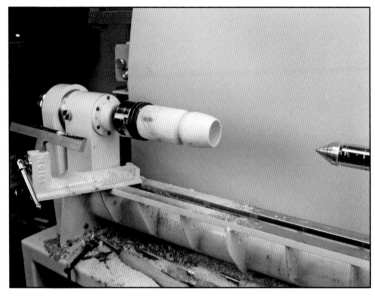

The cup is hollowed and ready for sanding. Note: don't make the cup deeper than your longest finger or you won't be able to sand the finished product. My limit happens to be 3 inches.

Next use a round-nose scraper, starting from the center and sweeping out to the rim. Remember to hold the scraper at an angle as demonstrated. This allows expulsion of the tool in case of a catch. If one holds it tip up instead of tip down a catch will cause a severe dig-in and scoop destruction.

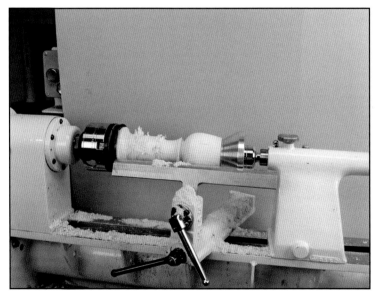

Bring up the tailstock cone and begin to shape the cup base and handle.

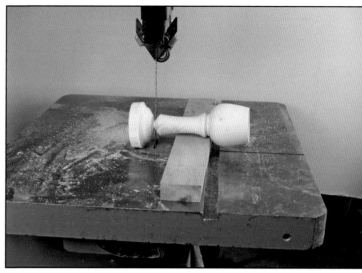

Remove the scoop and cut the handle from the base with a fine-toothed blade. Support the handle with a wooden slat.

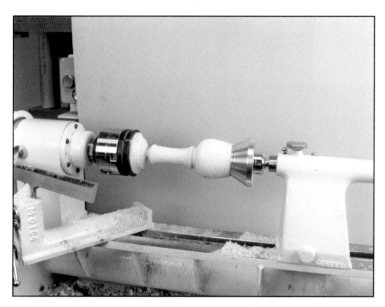

The scoop handle is turned and ready for sanding.

The cut surface may be hand sanded.

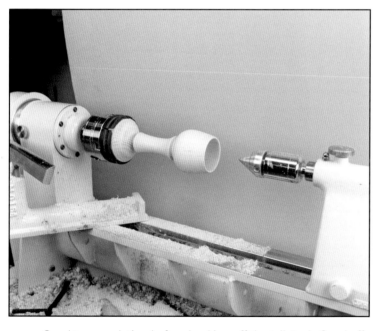

Sand to completion before backing off the tailstock. Sand off any marks left behind from the cone.

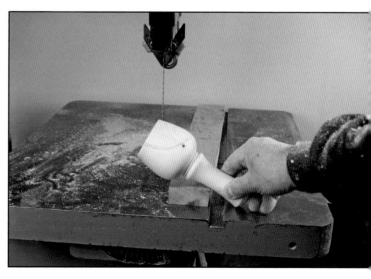

Mark on the cup the approximate area to be removed.

Cut out the marked area by pulling it through the band saw instead of pushing it through. The cut surface may be sanded on a small bench top belt sander to remove band saw cut marks. The scoop may be left plain or one may apply some walnut oil as a finish.

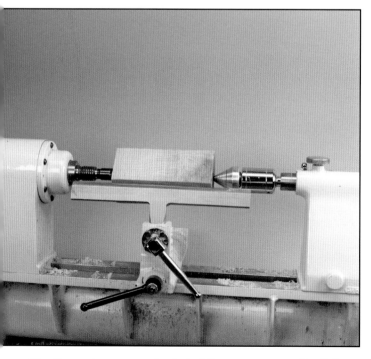

The Berger-type scoop is started the same way as the Raffan scoop, that is, a 2-1/2 x 2-1/2 x 8-inch piece is mounted between centers.

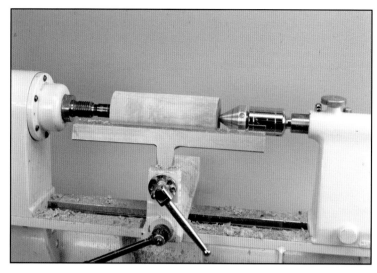

Turn the stock to a cylinder.

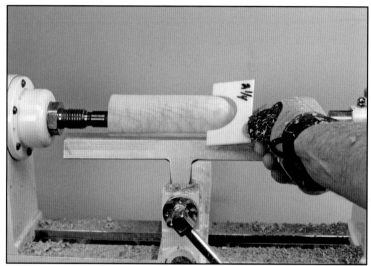

Begin forming a sphere using the 3/8-inch spindle gouge. A piece of cut plastic or cardboard with the desired diameter is most helpful.

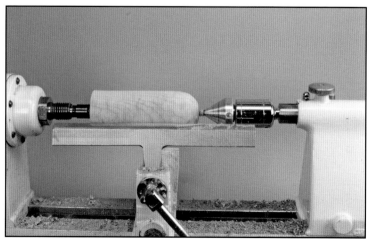

Make sure the hemisphere is turned away from the point mark leaving a small nubbin.

Recheck the roundness of the hemisphere before continuing. If the form is off, continue turning to gain a true hemisphere.

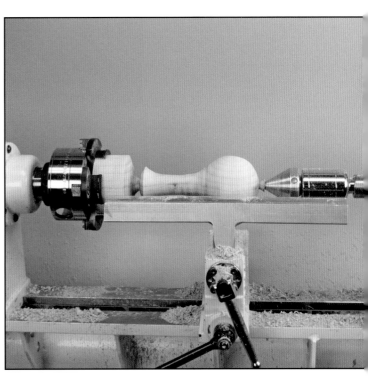

Shape a handle to your liking. I like a thin, delicate handle, but my wife always complains that my handles are too small and hard to hold. This scoop has a large clumsy handle.

Begin turning the other half of the sphere using the template guide.

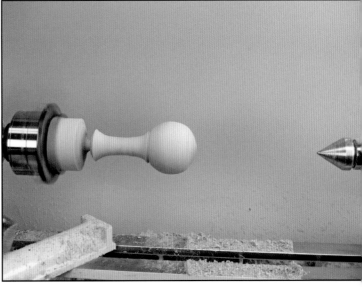

Back off the tailstock and turn off the nubbin.

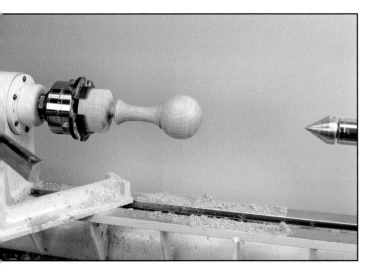

Sand to completion.

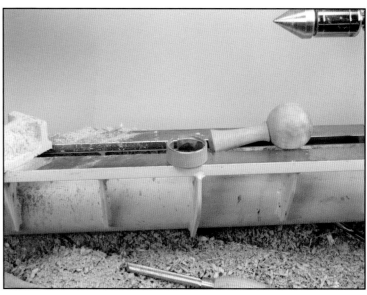

The scoop is ready to be mounted for further turning. Notice the cut ring used for mounting. Soren Berger has made these specifically for his scoops. The ring fits nicely into the #2 Talon jaws or equivalent chuck.

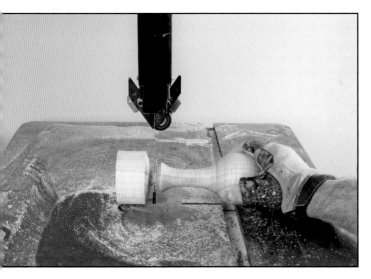

Cut off the base on a band saw.

Push the ball of the scoop into the ring and tighten the jaws. If one has turned a perfect sphere the ring will hold with its subtle interior dovetail. Whenever mounting the sphere place the handle at a slight angle towards the tool rest. This will give a finished scoop that allows one to use it without getting fingers into flour or sugar.

Hold the sphere firmly to prevent the scoop from spinning when cutting. Sand the cut surface smooth.

Before starting the lathe check the swing of the handle to make sure it clears the tool rest. Also note that the speed needs to be about 3000 rpms since the base of the scoop handle will be turned. If one were an expert turner, one could turn the backside of the handle, re-mount it and turn the front side as well. For our project we will not do this because of dangers involved. Make sure eye protection and a face shield is worn. It is also wise to add some weight to a shelf or the legs of the lathe for added support since the pieced is off-centered when rotating.

Approximate the depth needed for 3/16-inch wall thickness and use the depth gauge to get the correct depth.

Begin hollowing out the scoop starting at the center and working back with the ½- or ¼-inch bowl gouge. Remember this is cross grain hollowing just like one does for bowls.

Finish by using the ¼-inch bowl gouge to obtain the proper wall thickness. Notice the flute is closed upon entry. As one passes along the interior wall, one opens the flute towards the bottom.

Some may wish to use a scrapper to remove tool marks, but some grain tear out will occur in the cross grain piece making sanding somewhat difficult.

Sand the piece to completion and remember to keep the sanding hand behind the tool rest extending the finger into the scoop cup. Remember there is a club handle rotating at 3000 rpms and contact with a finger or hand spells pain. After the scoop is removed from the ring, sand off the ring marks.

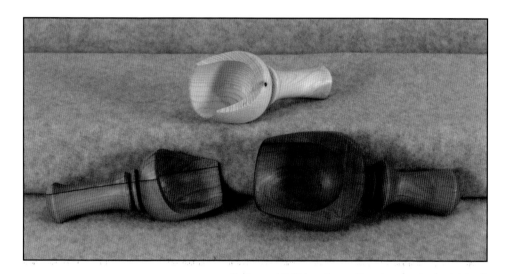

Three Raffan scoops are noted, the front 2 made from left over cherry and the back one of fir.

Three Berger-type scoops are noted, far left of fir and the other two of curly maple.

Chapter 2
Turned Cylinder Box

Many years ago, when I was first learning how to turn properly, Ray Key was my first mentor. We made cylinder, capsule, and finial topped friction-fitted, lidded boxes in his classes. It was most fun and still brings back pleasant memories in spite of all the time that has passed. Turned cylinder, friction-fitted, lidded boxes are really quite easy to construct from dense grain timbers. They yield a delightful end product, able to be utilized for gifts or hold that special piece of jewelry for a memorable occasion. More than once my wife has received rings, bracelets, or pins in one of the boxes.

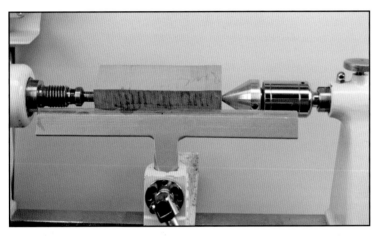

A nice size box may be constructed out of 2 x 2-inch stock. The piece mounted between centers came from some left-over Swiss pear wood that was used for another project. Most of the pieces were about 6 inches long, slightly longer than what was needed, but long enough to yield 2 boxes of different sizes.

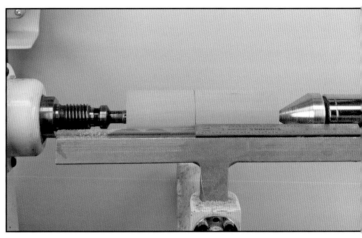

Measure in from the tailstock end about 3 inches and make a circumferential pencil line.

Turn the stock to a cylinder and square the ends with a parting tool.

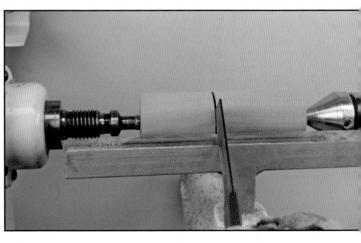

Using a narrow parting tool, cut in to create a ½-inch dowel.

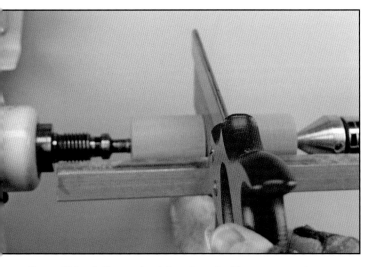

Turn off the lathe and cut the dowel with a cross-cut saw.

Mount the 3-inch long, 2-inch diameter piece in the #2 O'Donnell jaws. Turn the piece true with a ½-inch skew and re-square the end.

Measure in about one inch to part off the top portion. The magic number for the proper ratio of lid to bottom is about 2/5ths to 3/5ths; this would make the bottom 1-1/2 inches. After the allowances for forming the friction-fitted lid onto the base the near exact ratio for the golden mean (1.618) will be met for the base to lid.

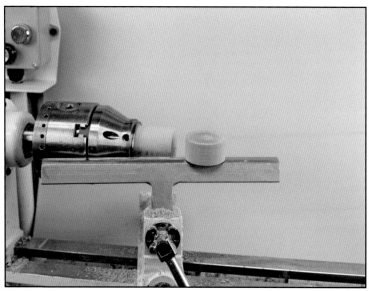

The parted off lid is ready for mounting and hollowing.

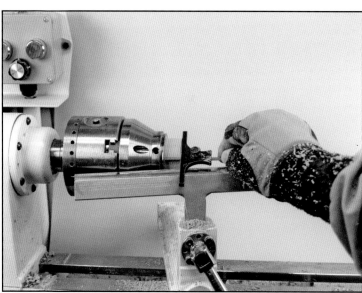

Mount the lid—parted off side towards the tailstock—in the #2 O'Donnell jaws and adjust the depth gauge to just meet the jaws. This will give 3/16-inch for the lid top thickness.

Using the Ray Key hollowing tool (a modified ½-inch spindle gouge) push in at dead center to drill a ½-inch deep hole.

Continue to remove material until the depth gauge touches the bottom when resting on the lid rim.

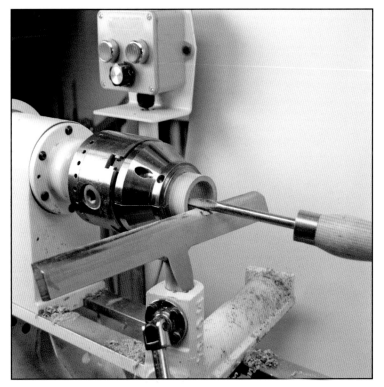

Begin sweeping out to the periphery with the flute at 45 degrees, leaving a wall thickness slightly proud of 3/16 inches.

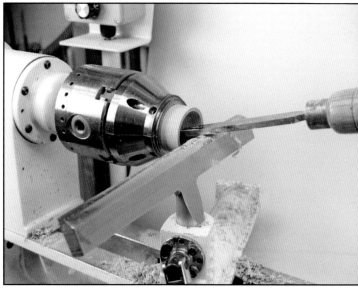

Next, use a straight scraper held at an angle to finish the bottom flat and the sides straight and smooth. It is best to have a subtle curve on the outside edge of the scraper to give a smooth transition from the inside lid top to the side.

Use a ¼-inch square rebate tool with its tip and part of the outside edge sharpened to cut the ¼-inch deep sleeve.

Buff with waxed 0000 steel wool.

Notice the cut sleeve or rebate is half the thickness of the wall. This is done so that, when the spigot is formed for the base to fit into the top, the inside top and bottom lines will be as straight as the outside surfaces.

Sand with 150 to 320 grit waxed sandpaper after applying some decorative rings with the skew.

A finish like lacquer or polyurethane may be applied to the finished inside. If lacquer is used, friction dry it with a cloth.

Next mount the bottom portion in the O'Donnell jaws and, using the ¼-inch rebate tool, cut a spigot to fit into the lid.

Use the thin parting tool to cut a slight line 1/32-inch wide and 1/32-inch deep to define the lid and base junction. Use the tip of the skew to cut a subtle incline at the edge of the top and place several lines for decoration.

Several practice tries are sometimes needed to get a good firm fit. Also, start with a small spigot until the proper fit is obtained then widen it to the correct distance to fit in the rebate. Don't have the fit too tight or the lid will crack at the thin 3/32-inch rim. If the lid is too loose one won't be able to turn the top to completion, but will have to start over making the spigot. Also note that whenever the bottom portion of the box is hollowed out the lid will become slightly looser.

Use the skew to smooth the lid and base, then sand to completion as was done for the lid's interior. Apply a finish of choice.

Remove the lid and hollow out the base to the same thickness as the lid.

Use the depth gauge to obtain the proper box depth.

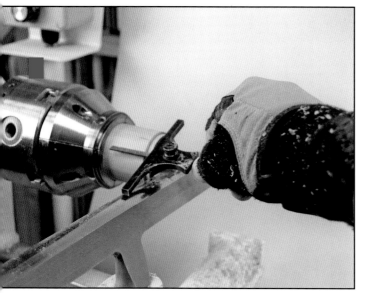

When calculating the depth, try to account for enough space to part off the base at the jaws and allow 3/16-inch for the bottom thickness.

Use the rounded-over square scrapper to smooth the bottom and sides.

Sand the interior to completion and apply the finish of choice.

Check the fit of the lid after hollowing and make necessary adjustments as needed—one can only remove material not replace any.

The finished base is ready to have its bottom turned.

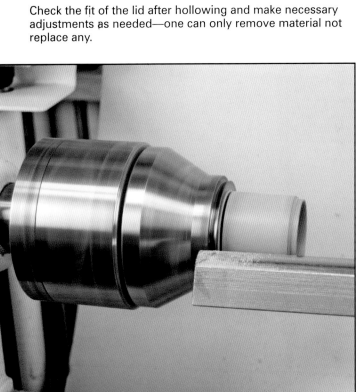

Using the narrow parting tool, part off the finished base.

If one used a longer piece of pear wood, a jam fit chuck could be fashioned to fit the bottom inside. Here a piece of she oak is turned down to fit into the base.

Check the fit to make sure it is firm but not too tight. Turn the jam chuck so that the thin-walled base doesn't crack.

Push on the base to finish its bottom.

Using a ½-inch skew, cut a subtle concavity on the bottom and place some design lines.

Notice the subtle concavity. Remember there is not much material between the inside and outside.

Sand the bottom to completion and apply a finish of choice.

Notice the fine detail on the top and bottom portions of the box.

Notice the fine detail of the interior of the top and bottom pieces.

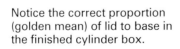

Notice the correct proportion (golden mean) of lid to base in the finished cylinder box.

Chapter 3
Off-Centered Handles

Constructing off-centered handles is an interesting technique first brought to my attention by Petter Herud, a most artistic Norwegian who happens to turn. Oval handles are used for tools, cutlery, sliding glass doors, and other sundry sorts of hand held objects. The tapered, oval handle feels and looks much better than a round one. The process is usually accomplished on a large, heavy lathe because of the speeds required to turn objects out of balance. The stock is in contact with the roughing gouge only about 1/6th of each revolution. The high rpms (usually over 3000) are necessary to have the off-centered stock appear to the tool's cutting edge as a solid object. I've found turning shorter handles for cutlery off-centered can be carried out on mini-lathes or smaller lathes especially if sand bags, concrete, or lead shot is used for ballast. Another trick is to have a friend stand—out of the line of fire—on the legs to dampen the vibrations.

The turned, oval handle has 3 centers, one for each side of the oval and one for the rounded center portion. Since most tangs are also oval, a rounded drilled hole will not work for its insertion. The fork or knife would merely spin in the drilled hole. Instead, an oblong cut hole is necessary to firmly hold the tang. This may be accomplished by cutting an opening in a slat the exact thickness of the tang. The stock handles seem to work best if they are about 1-½ inches thick and about 1-¾ inches wide.

Measure the thickness of the tang with an accurate measuring device that can measure in metric or thousandths of an inch. The thickness of the tang is exactly 230 thousandths of an inch.

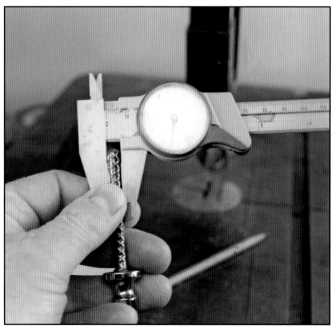

Measure the width of the tang. It is 250 thousandths or ¼-inch.

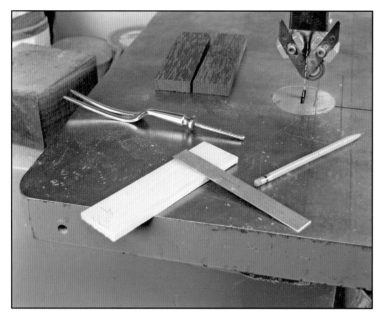

We are using black palm for the handle and yellow heart for the center accent piece. Black palm is very good for cutlery even though it is somewhat difficult to turn off-centered. The black palm has a propensity to have surface irregularities making it easy to grip with greasy hands when carving meat. The yellow heart needs to be the exact thickness (230 thousandths) of the tang. This can be accomplished by running 1-¾-inch wide pieces through the planer until the proper thickness is reached. The handle should be about 6 to 6-½ inches long so the yellow heart would be 1-¾ inches wide, 6 inches long, and 230 thousandths thick. This would mean each black palm piece should be about 1-¾ inches wide, 6 inches long, and about 5/8 inches thick. Find the center point of the yellow heart and draw a line down it.

Mark a line 1/8 inch on either side of the center points and 5/16 inch longer than the tang. Carefully cut out the marked portion on the band saw.

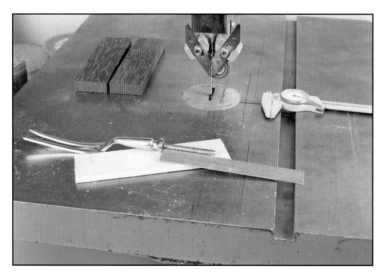

Measure the length of the tang. One should add about ¼ to 5/16 inch to the length to account for glue (we usually use a thick epoxy) as well as squaring of the ends on a chop saw in case there is movement with the glue-up.

Check the fit to make sure it is tight before proceeding to the other pieces. If the fit is OK and one is making several sets use the cut piece for a pattern, checking the fit after each is cut out.

Do the same measurements for the knife tang and cut more yellow heart slats.

After all the pieces are cut we are ready for the glue-up. Use a good glue like Titebond III so there is enough working time. Be careful not to get any glue in the cut opening for the tang.

After applying the glue flip over the slat and press it into place. Apply glue to the next surface being careful not to get spill over into the opening.

Press together the black palm and yellow heart pieces.

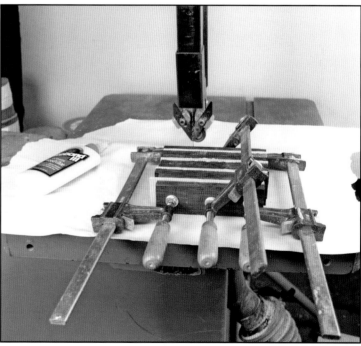

After several pieces are glued together clamp the handles together to dry—about 24 hours. Whenever the pieces are dry square the ends on a chop saw. It is most important to have the ends square for the off-center mounting.

For illustrative purposes we are using cherry with a blood-wood accent because it is easier to see the markings and photograph. Measure the thickness of the glue-up.

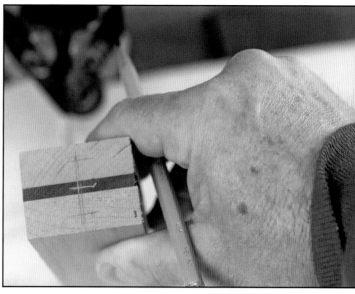

Use the same procedure on the other end, that is, draw a line through the half way point of the piece, measure in 7 mm from each side and draw a line. Measure the half-way thickness of the bloodwood and draw a line. All the crosses are points for mounting in both headstock and tailstock.

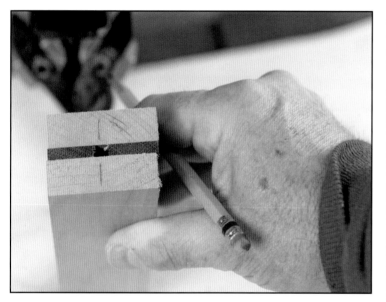

Divide the thickness in half and mark lines on the ends.

Measure in from the sides about 7 mm and draw a line on each side—remember the sharpened pencil line is about .5 mm thick.

Use a punch to mark the cross points on either side.

With a ¼-inch drill (slightly larger than the hole size) make a 1/8- or 3/16- inch deep hole.

The round hole will be used for mounting with the round live center. If one tries to mount an oblong opening there could be slippage and an irregular oval would be created.

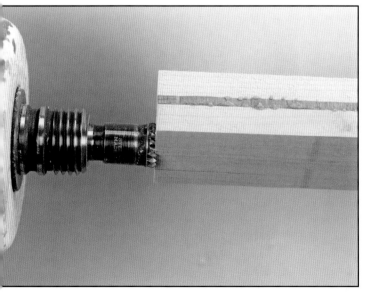

Using the previously made punch marks, place the stock on the lathe.

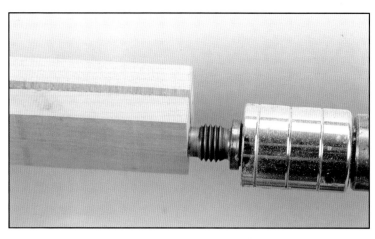

Use the cup center with its point in place and tightly advance the cup center so that marks are left behind.

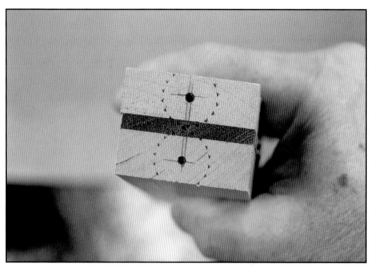

Do the same for the other punch hole set so that good centering marks are made for the headstock mounting.

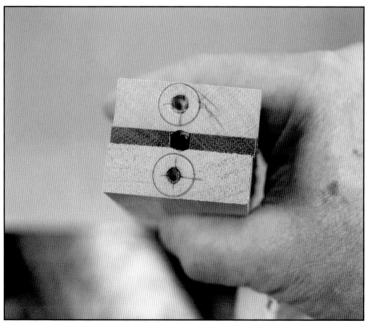

Notice the cup marks for mounting at the tailstock end.

Mount the black palm piece in the previously marked holes. Manually turn the stock to make sure it clears the tool rest before turning on the lathe. Run the lathe at 3000 rpms.

Remove the stock, the steb center, and the live center.

A close-up shows the "ghost" and the yellow heart center. Using the roughing gouge, turn the ghost down to the yellow heart.

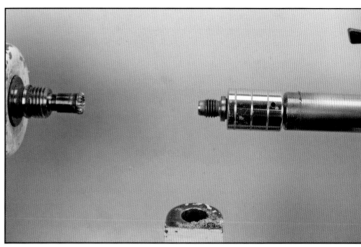

This step is very very important. Knock out the center points from both steb and cup centers.

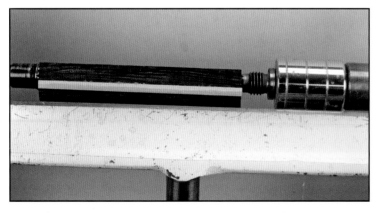

Stop the lathe and check to see that the oval is turned to the center of the yellow heart on either side.

Remount the stock in the steb center and cup center holes to turn the flat surface oval on the other side.

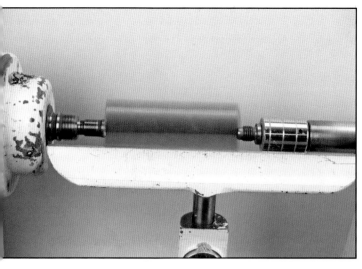

Turn down to the yellow heart while carefully watching the ghost.

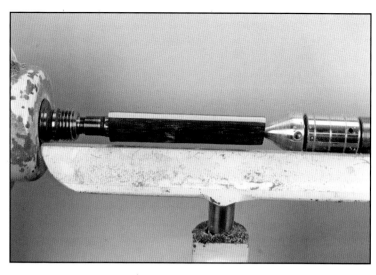

Remount the oval handle by its center points and replace the point center at the tailstock and the point center of the steb center.

When the yellow heart is reached, stop the lathe.

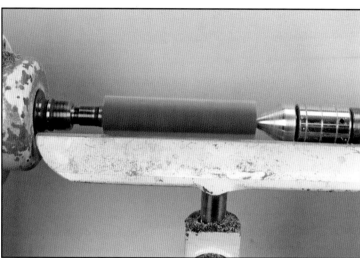

Turn the stock, rounding over the yellow heart with the roughing gouge.

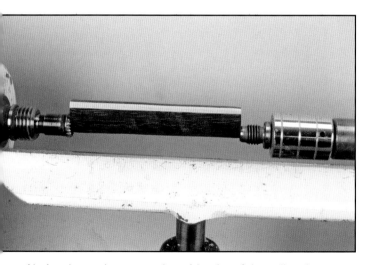

Notice the oval meets at the mid point of the yellow heart center.

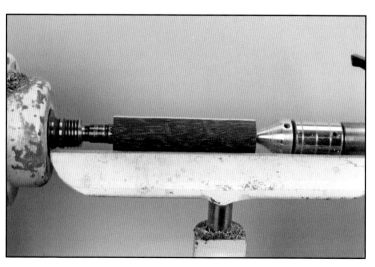

Check the stock before shaping the handle.

Round over the backside and front side of the handle using a 3/8-inch spindle gouge.

Measure the long axis of the oval stop on the fork beyond the tang and turn the taper to that size. Sand using 80 to 320 grit sandpaper, holding the folded strips to either side of the stock so that one's hands are free of the rotating irregularly shaped wood.

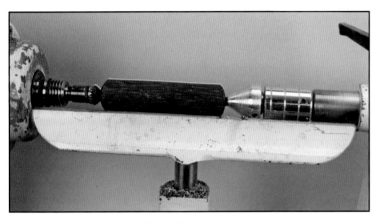

Turn a taper towards the front of the handle.

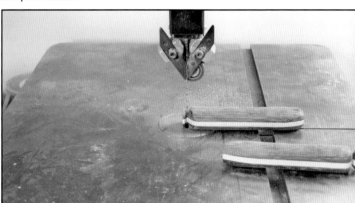

Remove the oval handle, cut off the headstock nubbin, and lightly sand the cut point. Finish the handles with wipe-on polyurethane. Use thick epoxy on the tang to glue in the fork and knife.

Two lovely sets of cutlery with black palm and yellow heart finished with polyurethane. The bread knife with cherry and bloodwood is the one demonstrated for the punch markings.

Chapter 4
Lidded Bowls with Foil Leaf

Lidded bowls are fun articles to construct out of nearly any stock that is about 5 inches square and 3 inches thick. I first learned how to make them about 15 years ago when taking a course from Richard Raffan. The idea of using foil leaf comes from Jimmy Clewes and his many clever artistic embellishments to interesting turnings.

While digging through the bowels of my wood storage shed, I came across a number of Oregon walnut and maple burl blanks. Cutting away check marks yielded a few pieces 5 x 5 x 3 inches for the project.

Mark a pencil line about 1-¾-inch in from one side and cut the squared piece on the band saw.

Cut out the discs. If the wood happens to be wet and needs drying one could tape together the non-cut surfaces with masking tape and set the stock aside for 6 months. In this instance the maple burl is dry and ready to go.

Next, use a compass to draw a circle on the cut surfaces of the 1-¾-inch thick and 1-¼-inch thick pieces. Mark the compass center point with an X for drilling later on. We want the cut surfaces to meet so that the grain pattern flows through the piece.

Drill a ¼-inch diameter, ¾-inch deep hole in the center of the cut surface of the base (the thicker portion of wood).

Mount the disc (bowl stock) on the Glaser screw chuck and square the bottom.

Use the 3/8-inch spindle gouge to cut a 1/8-inch thick foot to fit the O'Donnell jaws.

With calipers, mark a 2-inch area for the foot to fit the O'Donnell jaws.

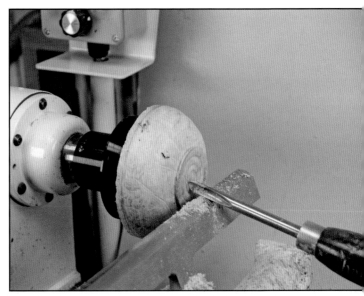

Roll some beads on the foot's bottom surface with the 3/8-inch spindle gouge.

Using the ½-inch bowl gouge (52 degree bevel) begin to shape the bowl with push cuts.

Continue shaping the bowl with the bowl gouge to create a rolled over appearance at the rim (closed form bowl).

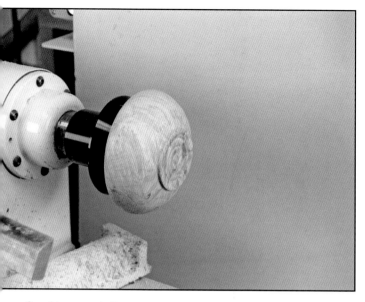

Sand to completion.

Notice the ½-inch bowl gouge with a 72 degree double-bevel cut for finishing the bottom of the bowl. Note: a double bevel allows smooth transition from side to bottom without getting a catch when the flute is completely opened.

Mount the bowl's foot with a firm, but not tight, grip in the O'Donnell jaws.

Start removing stock by cutting towards the center and working back to the rim with the ½-inch, 52 degree bevel cut bowl gouge.

Notice the 3/8-inch bowl gouge with a 40 degree bevel cut for cutting the interior of the rolled over rim of the bowl.

As more wood is removed it is most difficult to cut the inside rim with the ½-inch, 52 degree bevel bowl gouge.

Switch to the 40 degree bevel, 3/8-inch bowl gouge to carefully cut the inside of the rolled over rim. Notice the flute is closed with the sharply angled entry cut.

Use the 72 degree double-beveled, ½-inch bowl gouge to smooth out the bottom and make a non-noticeable transition from the side cuts to the bottom cuts. The entire bowl should be about 3/16 inches thick.

Power sand the inside using 2-inch green discs, 100 to 400 grits. If your lathe has a reverse switch reverse the directions between grits. Remember to touch the lower end of the revolving sanding disc whenever the stock is turning towards the front and the reverse for reverse rotation. After the power sanding is complete remove the bowl and begin work on the lid.

Since the lid is about 5 inches in diameter, it fits nicely into #4 Oneway jaws for turning. However, other means of mounting could be utilized if one so desired. With the lid in the jaws square the bottom with the ½-inch bowl gouge.

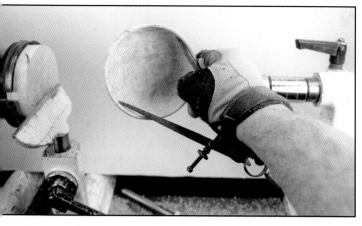

Measure the inside opening of the finished bowl with calipers.

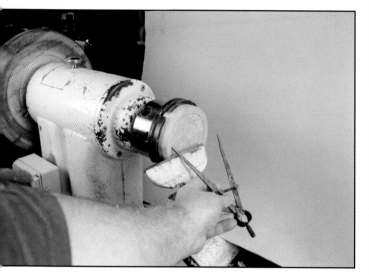

Mark that diameter on the bottom surface of the lid. Also, measure the outside diameter of the Talon #2 jaws (2-1/4 inches) and mark that diameter on the lid base as well. It is important to plan to have enough material between the fit in the bowl and the fit in the jaws so that the jaws don't fracture the ring when expansion pressures are applied.

Turn the outside rim true, taper a slight cove to the ¼-inch deep spigot to fit the bowl and, finally, turn a ¼-inch rebate to fit the Talon jaws. One may make a pointed nubbin in the center for design.

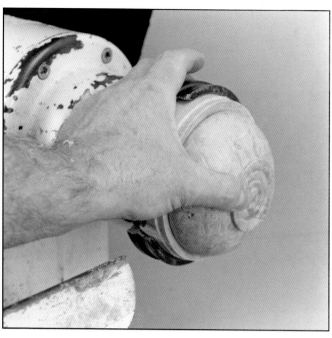

Check the fit of the bowl. It should be rather loose.

With the 1/2-inch skew, add some design lines.

Sand the inside surface to completion.

Mount the lid on the Talon chuck with the #2 jaws in expansion mode. Use a firm but not tight grip.

Begin shaping a dovetailed center 1-1/4"-inch handle with a 3/8-inch rise.

Try to make the curve produced by the closed form bowl rim appear to flow into the lid. Add a recessed bead and turn a slight concavity in the center knob before adding some cut lines for decorations.

Sand the lid to completion.

After the bowls are completed, apply wipe-on polyurethane satin finish to all surfaces except the interior of the bowl. Buff with 0000 steel wool to remove any dust defects then apply the acrylic base coat to the interior of the bowl where the foil will be applied. Use a good brush.

Apply the base coat to all bowls which will receive foil leaf. The base coat is latex-based so that the brush may be cleaned with water. The base coat dries in about 20 minutes and is ready for application of the acrylic adhesive. Remember to shake the adhesive before the application.

The key to application is to wear disposable surgical gloves that have talc on them. This helps to keep the foil from adhering to the fingers and makes it less difficult to press foil onto the adhesive.

With another good brush, apply the adhesive to the bowl's interior. Make sure to smooth over any irregularities of the adhesive. The adhesive will have a milky appearance when wet. Since the adhesive is water-based latex brushes may be cleaned with water.

Sometimes the foil will crack open when pressed into the concavity of the bowl, leaving the red base coat apparent. Merely pressing another piece of foil onto the crack will resolve the problem. If one has difficulty covering some cracks, more adhesive may be applied. Remember to let it partially dry—about 20 minutes—before applying more leaf.

When it is partially dry, the adhesive will appear shiny clear and is ready for foil application. It takes only 20 minutes for the adhesive to dry to this point.

Some foil comes as flakes and may be easily pressed into the bowl as noted in the bowl on the right. Some foil, like the silver leaf, comes in sheets that are ultra-thin and may be applied as noted in the center bowl.

Notice the small bowl in the back. Leaf that is 22 karat gold has been applied to it. The 22 karat gold leaf is quite thin and difficult to work. If one takes a 1-inch cube of gold and pounds it out to the size of a football field, it will have the thickness of gold leaf.

Green leaf, a slightly thicker product than 22 karat gold leaf, is much easier to apply. It is a combination of nickel, copper, and other metals, all of which will tarnish when oxidized.

Various defects are much easier to cover up than with the plain leaf.

The next step is to mount the bowl and, using a sable brush, lightly brush against the grain to remove non-adhering specks of leaf. It is best to do this in both forward and reverse directions, but should one's lathe not have a reverse the brushing may be done freehand.

Experimentation with a goat hair brush (about ¼ the cost of sable) yields adequate cleansing of foil specks.

Buff the rim of the bowl with 0000 steel wool to remove any base coat, adhesive, or foil.

A second buffing with the goat hair brush will remove any left-over residue.

Notice how the curve of the bowl flows into the lid, presenting a pleasing effect.

The interior of the lidded bowls adds another pleasant surprise for its recipient. Remember to apply a spray-on acrylic clear finish to all non-karat gold foil to prevent tarnishing. Wear a painter's respirator as the spray finish is toxic. Use masking tape to cover the rim to prevent spill over of the finish. Always wait about 24 hours before applying the spray-on acrylic clear finish, to allow complete drying of the adhesive.

Chapter 5
Christmas Ornaments

Making Christmas tree ornaments is a fun project no matter what the time of year. A similar article "Twisted Icicles" appeared in American Woodturner in the winter 2006 issue, but the pictures and text are different here. However, the techniques and ideas are the same.

The original idea of using recycled Christmas trees comes from my friend Arnie. Over the years he has introduced me to junk yards, dumpster diving, and various dumps where the Christmas trees are thrown away. Usually in January we head off to the Christmas tree recycle dump and grab all the trees, cut off their branches with a hatchet—we're not allowed to used chain saws at the dump—and load up his pick-up truck. After storing them for about 6 months or so the trees are dry enough to turn. Nevertheless, one must wear old clothes, goggles, and gloves, because much sap sprays from the turning trunks.

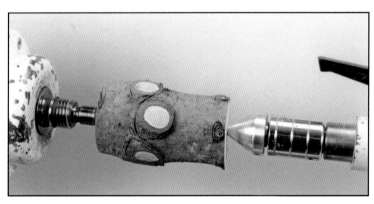

If one cuts off a piece of trunk where all the branches exit a better grain pattern will result in the ball of the ornament. Use a piece of trunk about 5 to 6 inches long and about 2-1/2 to 3 inches in diameter.

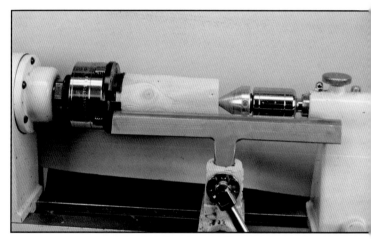

Mount the stock in the Talon chuck and tighten the jaws.

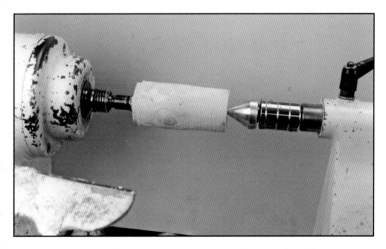

With a roughing gouge, turn the stock smooth and turn a spigot at the headstock end to fit the Talon #2 jaws or equivalent chuck.

Begin turning a sphere with a 3/8-inch spindle gouge.

Round over the tailstock end, but leave enough stock at the headstock end to be able to drill a 3/8-inch hole through the entire ball and still maintain adequate support.

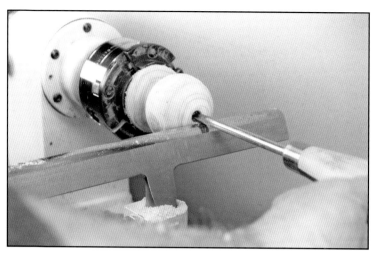

Begin hollowing with the straight tool stopping frequently to blow out the shavings with either compressed air or blowing through a straw.

With a 3/8-inch drill bit in a Jacobs chuck, drill a through-and-through hole at 200 rpms. Lubricate the drill bit with some beeswax.

After a channel is made begin using the curved hollowing tools and hollow the tailstock area first. Work back towards the headstock end.

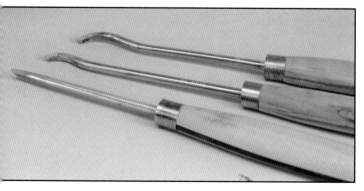

Several small hollowing tools are used to hollow out the ball. There is a straight blade, a one-half curve, and a full curve. These are available at most wood craft or turning stores.

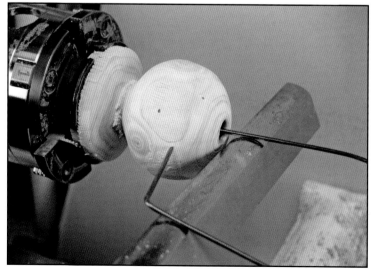

A bent coat hanger acts as a depth and thickness gauge during the procedure (a clever Dick Sing invention).

Make sure the gap is about ¼-inch.

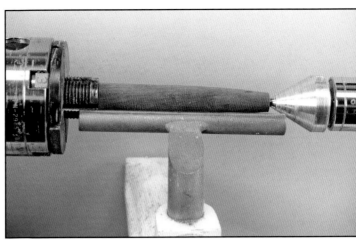

When preparing the icicle stock between centers, turn a spigot to fit the #1 jaws of the Talon chuck. Mount in the #1 jaws a tapered turned 6-1/2-inch piece of Honduran red heart for the icicle—red always seems to be the most desirable color for Christmas ornament icicles.

After the ball is hollowed to ¼-inch, sand it to completion, then part off the ball at the headstock end. Measure the opening with calipers so that the icicle dowel may be turned to the correct diameter to fit.

Use a narrow (1/8-inch) parting tool to cut a dowel near the headstock, leaving enough material to make the cap for the ornament.

The ball may be slid onto a tapered dowel to turn smooth the parted area. Finish by sanding the turned area.

Take the previous measurement from the ball's opening to size the dowel.

Begin forming a cove with an attached thickened ring, using the 3/8-inch spindle gouge.

Sand the ring with waxed sandpaper as was done for the other projects.

With a sharpened discarded dental pick, begin undercutting the ring.

Use the dental tool to part off the captive ring and clean up the parted area.

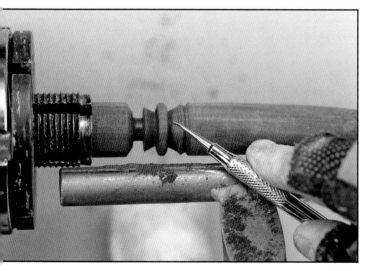

Undercut the other side, but be careful not to cut all the way through.

Continue shaping the icicle, making a small ball and spindle for twists.

Mark 12 start lines on the ball with a blue pencil, using the lathe's indexing system.

Take the 1/16-inch tungsten carbide, 80 grit rasp and begin carefully cutting along the pink pencil lines.

Draw pitch lines on the sphere.

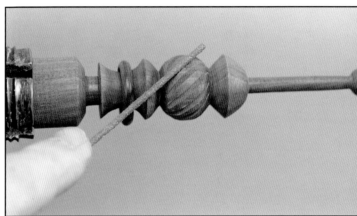

Cut along all the pencil lines, then go back over to smooth and even up the coves.

Using a pink pencil, draw lines from the lower left hand corner of one trapezoid to the upper right hand corner following into the next trapezoid towards the tailstock. Do the same for the remaining 11 trapezoids. The pink lines are the cut lines for a left-handed twist.

Next mark start lines on the thin spindle. Since we are doing a double barley, right-handed twist, mark start lines at 6, 12, 18, & 24 on the spindle.

Mark the pitch lines. Since the spindle thickness is 3/16-inch, mark the pitch lines every 3/8-inch and divide in half twice.

Sand the completed coves on the sphere, using torn pieces of Vitex pliable sandpaper twisted into 1/16-inch ropes 120, 150, 240, & 320 grits.

At one rectangle at the tailstock end draw a pink pencil line from the lower right hand corner to the upper left hand corner, continuing into the adjacent rectangle until the headstock end in reached. Do the same in the next second rectangle so that 2 cut lines are drawn. Note: For those with presbyopia, use 1.5 to 2 diopter lenses or other magnifying glasses.

Do the same for the spindle, but be very careful. After the sanding is complete on the twists, sand the remainder of the icicle to completion then turn the tip of the icicle to completion and sand the parted portion.

Carefully begin rasping with the 1/16-inch rasp to cut coves. Sometimes support with the free hand is helpful to prevent fracture of the delicate piece.

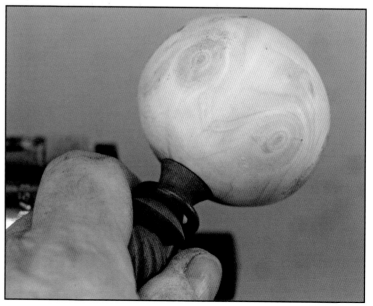

Use thick cyanoacrylate to glue the icicle into the sphere.

Next begin to shape the cap. Measure the opening at the top of the sphere and cut a dowel with a thin parting tool to fit the opening. Sand the top to completion, then drill a 1/16-inch hole at 200 rpms to fit the eyelet.

Screw in the eyelet with the lathe running slowly, part off the cap, then glue the cap onto the top of the ornament.

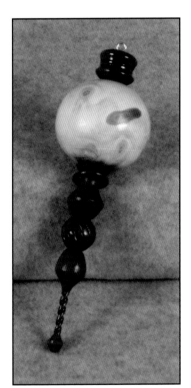

Finish the ornament with a gloss spray polyurethane finish. Remember to wear a painter's respirator and be careful not to over spray the captive ring area. Multiple light applications work best.

Several finished ornaments are displayed with ribbons.

Chapter 6
Pepper and Salt Mills

Pepper and salt mills are popular items to sell, make, or give as gifts. Most are somewhat difficult to construct on the smaller lathes, but with the advent of the crush grind mechanisms an easily constructed mill is readily at hand. Sizes may vary from 5 inches to 12 inches tall depending on the maker's preference. My bias is for the larger mills so we will demonstrate a 12-inch one—this is the tallest able to be constructed out of the crush grind mechanism.

If one uses left-over timber, run it through the planer to square the surfaces. Left over veneer yields interesting patterns as well. For this project left over cherry, yellow heart, 1/16-inch thick, black-dyed maple veneer and purple heart veneer were found in the wood shed. After the thick pieces were run though the planner they were glued together using polyurethane glue and clamped tight for 12 hours. The thickness was cut to about 3 inches, but glue-ups down to 2-1/2 inches could also be used for the 12 inch tall mills. Measure over 3 inches from one side and make a mark. Mark every 3 inches on both ends then draw a line from the corner to the first mark 3 inches over.

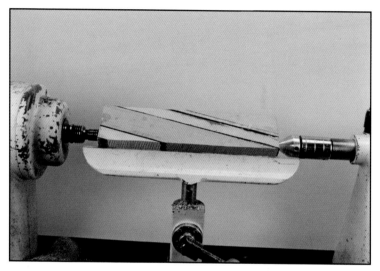

Square the ends of the stock with a chop saw and then mark the center points before mounting in the steb and live centers. The stock pieces should be slightly proud of 12 inches long.

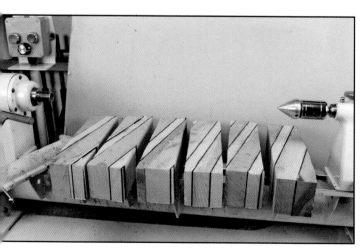

After all lines are drawn, cut along the lines on a band saw. This yields an interesting pattern for the stock. The two left over triangular end pieces may have their smooth sides glued together with veneer between to make another stock piece.

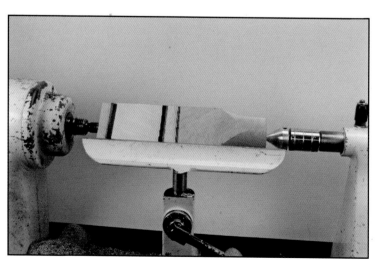

Using the roughing gouge begin to turn a cylinder.

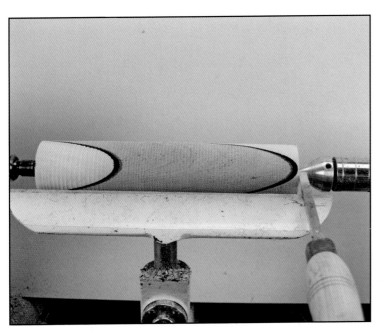

After a cylinder is formed, square the ends with a broad parting tool.

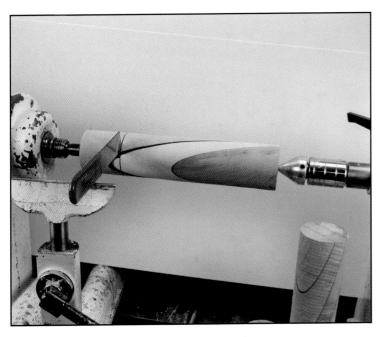

Measure in about 2-1/2 inches for the top and, using a narrow parting tool, cut to form an interior dowel of ¾ inches.

Turn off the lathe and use a crosscut saw to cut through the dowel separating the head from the base.

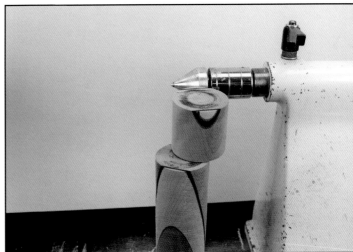

Mark matching numbers or letters on the cut surfaces if several mills are being made so that mismatches don't occur.

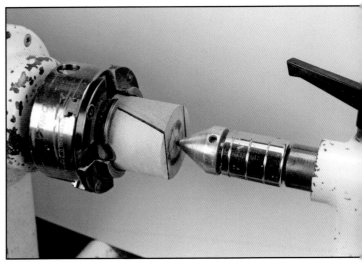

Mount the head in #2 Oneway jaws with the cut surface towards the tailstock. Square the bottom end.

Using a 15/16-inch Forstner bit drill a 1-1/4-inch deep hole at 200 rpms. Lubricate the bit with beeswax. The rebate will hold the crush mechanism's top stopper.

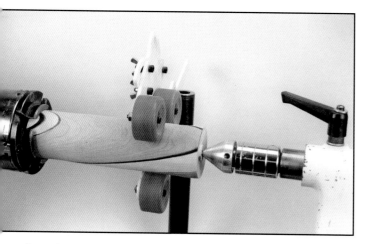

Set aside the drilled top and mount the base with the cut surface towards the headstock. Square the bottom end. Drilling the mills is more accurate if one uses a spindle steady. Many spindle steadies are commercially available, but one may construct their own without too much difficulty to fit the smaller lathe. If one doesn't use a spindle steady, drilling the large holes on long pieces becomes most difficult. The limit in height in my experience seems to be about a 7-inch mill.

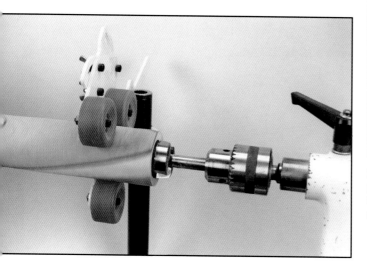

With a 1-¾ inch diameter Forstner bit, drill a 1-inch deep hole in the bottom. Lubricate the bit with beeswax.

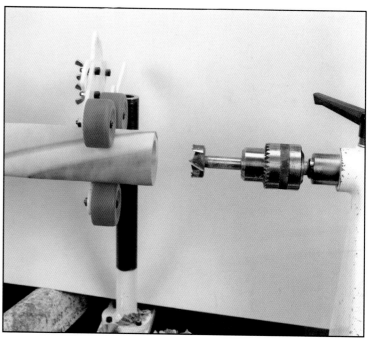

Next use a 1-9/16-inch diameter Forstner bit to drill a 1-½-inch deep hole. Lubricate the bit with beeswax. This hole will seat the crush mechanism.

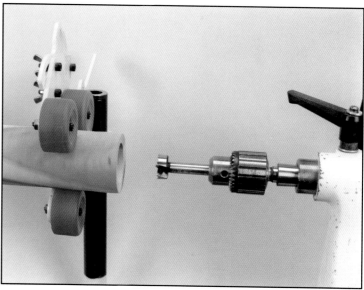

Use a 1-1/16 inch diameter Forstner bit to drill as deep as possible beyond the previously drilled hole. Lubricate the bit with beeswax. One may need to use a drill extension to get deep enough in the mill.

Notice the drilled holes and shelves created for the crush mechanism.

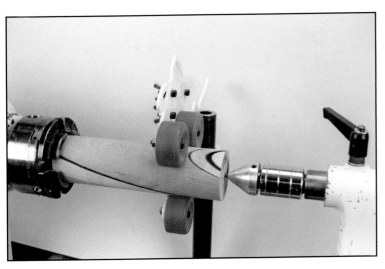

Reverse mount the stock after placing the appropriate number or letter (matching the top parted off portion) on the inside bottom of the 1-¾-inch diameter drilled hole. Square the end.

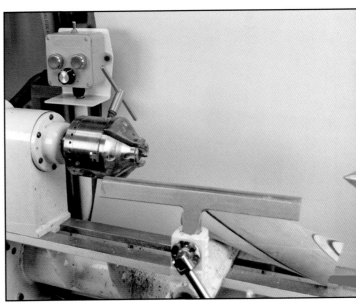

Use the 1-inch O'Donnell jaws to expansion-mount the base of the mill. Use a firm but not tight grip, so as to not fracture the thin wall of the mill.

Using the 1-1/16-inch Forstner bit, drill in to meet the drilled hole from the other end. The top stopper sleeve will seat in the drilled hole.

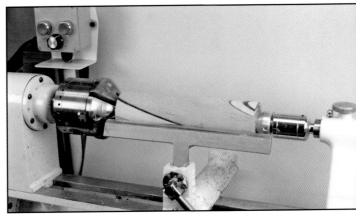

Bring up the tailstock in preparation for turning the mill.

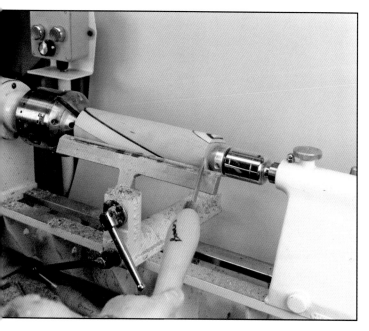

Use a ½-inch skew to re-square the top.

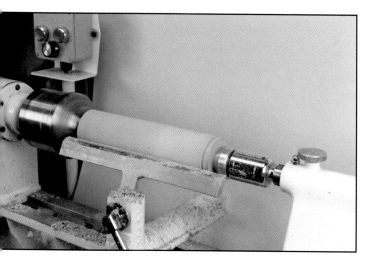

With the 3/8-inch spindle gouge, turn a bead at the top.

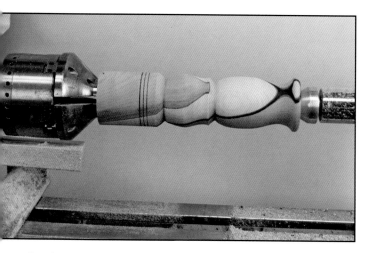

Continue to shape the mill, but remember not to cut too deeply at the bottom so that break-through into the drill holes doesn't occur.

Adding some twists to allow an easy grip will yield a lovely practical embellishment. Make sure there is a cove on either side of where the twists are to be carved; otherwise the rasp will foul on the bordering stock during production. Mark 12 blue start lines, utilizing the lathe's indexing system.

Draw 3 circumferential pitch lines, one in the middle and one at each end of the twist area.

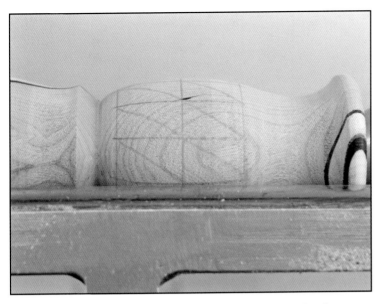

For a right-handed twist draw a pink fluorescent line from the lower right hand corner of one rectangle to the upper left hand corner and follow it into the next adjacent rectangle. Do the same for the other 11 rectangles.

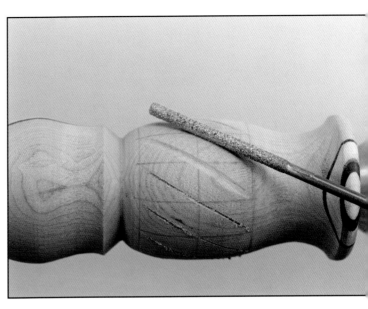

Using the 3/16-inch diameter, 60 grit tungsten carbide rasp, begin cutting coves along the cut marks.

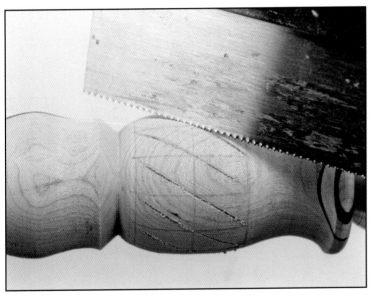

With a dovetail saw scarify along the pink fluorescent cut lines. Don't cut too deeply, but merely place a scar to guide the rasp.

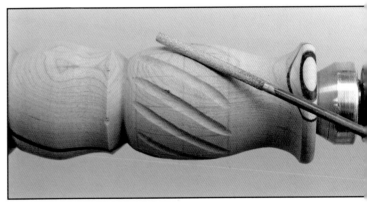

Continue cutting and shaping all 12 coves.

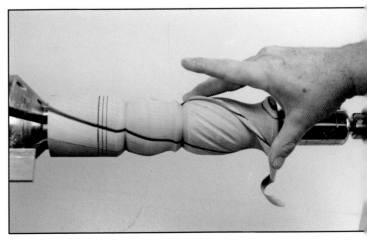

Sand the coves with tearable Vitex sandpaper twisted into ¼-inch ropes, 120, 150, 240, & 320 grits.

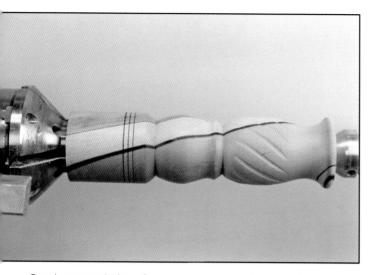

Sand to completion. One may have to re-turn any fractured or marred areas as noted in the photo above.

Make sure the head is mounted squarely, then begin turning a sphere.

Remove the base and use the Oneway small collet jaws to mount the 15/16-inch drilled hole in the head.

Turn another bead at the bottom to meet the base, then sand to completion.

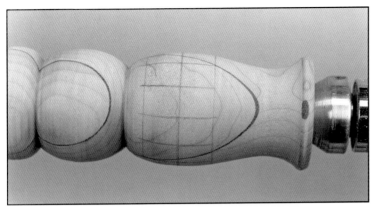

A companion mill for salt made out of lighter wood—left over curly maple pieces with purple heart veneer—makes a good mate if given an opposite twist. Using the indexing system mark 12 start lines then mark 3 pitch lines.

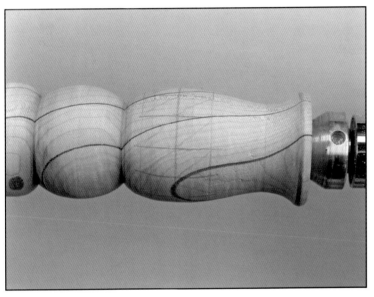

Draw a pink fluorescent line from the lower left hand corner of one rectangle to the upper right hand corner into the adjacent rectangle. Do the same for the other 11 rectangles. This gives the layout for a left-handed twist.

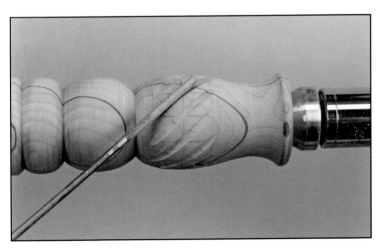

Use the 3/16-inch rasp after making saw cut scarifications to cut coves. Sand to completion as was done for the right-handed twists.

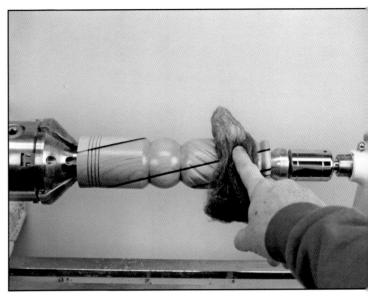

After several coats of wipe-on satin polyurethane are applied and dry, remount the base and buff with steel wool before applying a paste wax.

Do the same for the top.

Push the friction-fit top stopper into the drilled hole of the top.

Push the friction-fit crush grind mechanism into the bottom. Fit the top onto the metal rod and push the two pieces together. If the crush grind mechanism is pushed out, measure the distance on the aluminum rod and cut that much off the tip with a hack saw. Glue the stopper into the head and the crush grind mechanism into the base using epoxy.

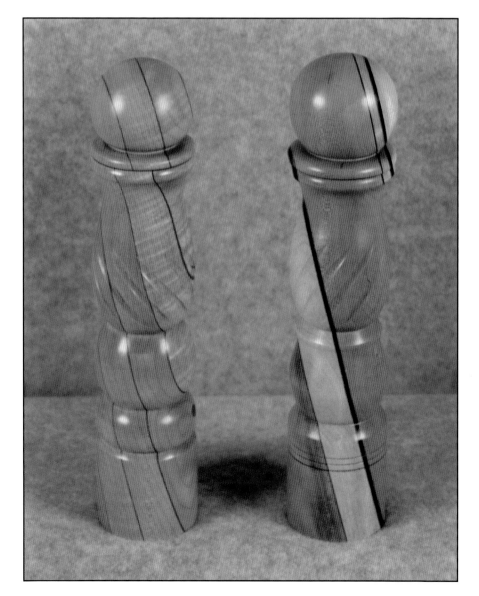

The 12-inch tall pair of salt and peppermills with left- and right-handed twists present attractive functional kitchenware.

Chapter 7
Gallery

Variously sized Raffan-type scoops.

Collection of Berger-type scoops.

Collection of various types of friction-fitted, lidded boxes of various timbers.

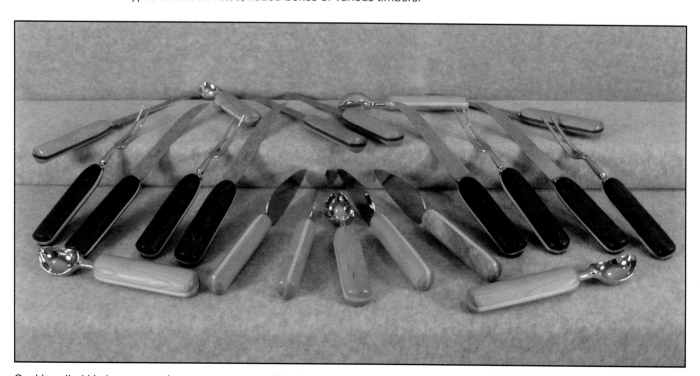

Oval handled kitchen ware—ice cream scoops with cherry & yellow heart, bread knives with cherry & bloodwood, pie knives with cherry & yellow heart, and carving sets with black palm & yellow heart.

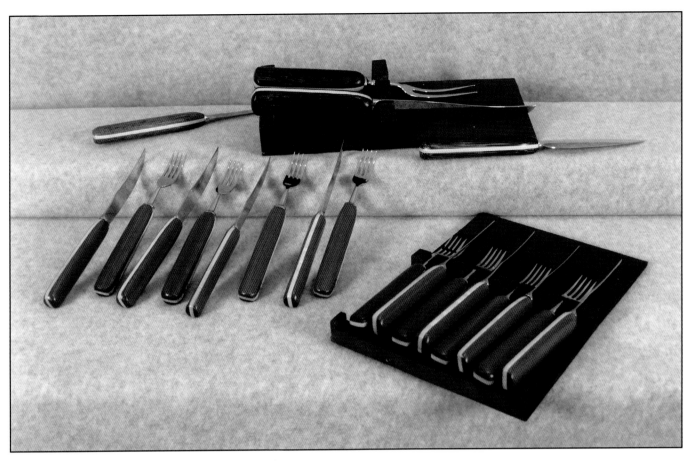

Steak knife and fork sets made from bloodwood and birds eye maple.

Lidded bowls of various timbers and different types of foil leafs.

Brass Christmas tree with recycled Christmas tree stock ornaments, red heart twisted icicles with captive rings; and banksia pod ornaments, some with twisted captive ring icicles in Jerusalem olivewood.

Pepper and salt mills, 12 inches tall with crush grind mechanisms and surface twists for better gripping.

Conventional 10-inch tall maple salt mills.

Stained maple 15-inch tall conventional peppermills with right- and left-handed twists.

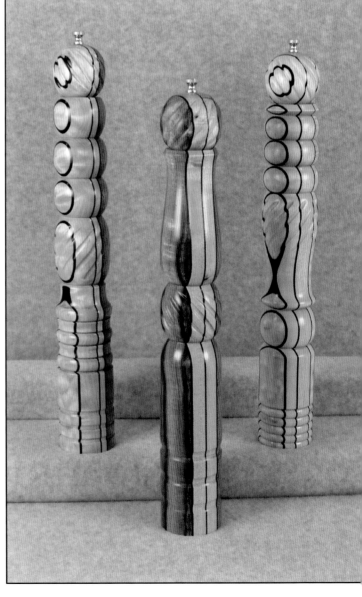

Straight cut, glue-up 19-inch tall conventional peppermills with twists on the top sphere as well as the body.

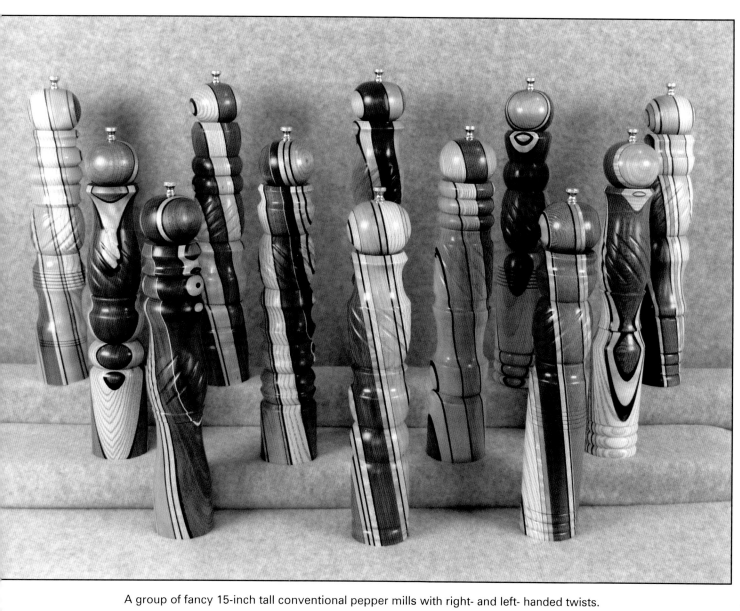

A group of fancy 15-inch tall conventional pepper mills with right- and left- handed twists.

Acknowledgments

Once again I would like to thank my wife Susan for tolerating my many hours of indulgence in turning, photographing, and composing text at the computer. My more than occasional outbursts of righteous indignation and expletives upon finding, creating, and causing errors have led to construction of many turned items for our church—probably her idea of my penance or just another way to get me on my knees at the altar. On the other hand, maybe she knows I'm just a soft touch whenever it comes to turning something for hope, faith, or charity. I also thank Burt Biss for his proofing of manuscript, pictures, and ideas; and Arnie Geiger for his dried and seasoned Christmas tree blanks as well as furthering my education (junk yards and dumpster diving). I would also like to thank Richard Raffan for his kind instructive guidance in past years, Soren Berger for his rings and ideas, Ray Key for his patience in teaching me proper techniques, Peter Herud for his nifty off-centered skills, and all the other turners who have inspired my talents. Last but not least, I would like to thank Jeff Trotter in helping take several photos where both my hands needed to be in the pictures. Special thanks go to my editor, Doug Congdon-Martin, whose comments, encouragement, and efforts make this book a success.